HENDERSON
CHILDREN'S

WINNIPEG
FEB 2 2005
✓
LIC LIBRARY

D0574523

WITHDRAWN

HENDERSON
CHILDREN'S

WINNIPEG
FEB 2 2005

AlphaBasiCs

Community Helpers
from A to Z

A Bobbie Kalman Book

 Crabtree Publishing Company

AlphaBasiCs

Created by Bobbie Kalman

For Nicole Pinch,
a true community helper

Editor-in-Chief
Bobbie Kalman

Writing team
Bobbie Kalman
Niki Walker

Research
Tara Harte

Managing editor
Lynda Hale

Editors
Niki Walker
Greg Nickles

Computer design
Lynda Hale
Robert MacGregor (cover concept)

Production Coordinator
Hannelore Sotzek

Special thanks to
Danielle, Peter, and Jordan Gentile and the St. Catharines Fire Department (the models who appear on the cover); Tracy Dixon; Allison and Amanda Vernal; Chris and Jason Miller; Mike Jacobs; Dina and Bessie Katsavelos; Chris Foo, Brad May, and the Futures Gymnastics Center; Janet Eastwood; Peter Koitsas; Paul Holder; Tajammal Majeed Qureshi; Lester Graham; Ramona Gellel; Jonathan Sacitharah; Karl and Priscilla Baker; Michael Malaney and Suki the dog; Dick Hyatt; Bill Carrey; Al Spicer and the West Lincoln Memorial Hospital ; Lauren McDonald; Stephanie Kostopoulos; Stacey and Angela Staios

Photographs
Animals Animals/Fritz Prenzel: page 31
Marc Crabtree: cover, title page, pages 7, 9 (top left), 11 (inset), 12, 17, 18, 20 (inset), 24, 25, 29 (right), 30 (both)
Bobbie Kalman: page 27
Ken Slingerland/Ontario Ministry of Agriculture, Food, and Rural Affairs: page 4
Jerry Whitaker: pages 11, 21, 28 (both), 29 (left)
Tony Zinnanti: pages 15, 20
Other images by Digital Stock, Digital Vision, and Image Club

Crabtree Publishing Company

350 Fifth Avenue
Suite 3308
New York
N.Y. 10118

360 York Road, RR 4
Niagara-on-the-Lake
Ontario, Canada
L0S 1J0

73 Lime Walk
Headington
Oxford OX3 7AD
United Kingdom

Copyright © **1998 CRABTREE PUBLISHING COMPANY.**
All rights reserved. No part of this publication may be reproduced, stored in a retrieval system or be transmitted in any form or by any means, electronic, mechanical, photocopying, recording, or otherwise, without the prior written permission of Crabtree Publishing Company.

Cataloging in Publication Data
Kalman, Bobbie
 Community helpers from A to Z

(AlphaBasiCs)
Includes index.

ISBN 0-86505-374-X (library bound) ISBN 0-86505-404-5 (pbk.)
This alphabet book explains the duties and importance of occupations geared toward the community, including emergency workers, medical workers, business people, and workers in the service industry.

1. Occupations—Juvenile literature. 2. Community—Juvenile literature. [1. Occupations. 2. Alphabet.] I. Title. II. Series: Kalman, Bobbie. AlphaBasiCs.

HT675.K35 1997   j331.7'02   LC 97-34894
                                            CIP

Contents

is for **agricultural workers**. Agricultural workers work on farms and help grow fruits and vegetables or raise livestock. Wherever you live, agricultural workers help your community. Few of us grow our own food, so we need farmers to grow it for us. Without agricultural workers, we would have no food to eat!

*Some agricultural workers own a farm, and some work for a farmer in their community. Others, called **migrant workers**, travel from place to place to help farmers in different areas.*

is for **business people**. If you look around your community, you will find many businesses. Grocery stores, car dealerships, restaurants, and banks are businesses. The people who own or run those places are very important to the community. They give people jobs and help the community in many other ways.

Take a walk in your neighborhood and write down the businesses you see. Make a list of all the ways these businesses help you, your community, and people in other communities.

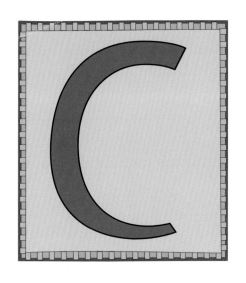

C is for **community helpers**. A community is a group of people who share services, buildings, and laws. It is also a place where people live. A community can be a school, town, city, or neighborhood. Community helpers make communities cleaner, safer, and more pleasant for other people.

A city is made up of many smaller communities. Some attract people that share a culture. Many of the community helpers in this neighborhood are Chinese.

C is also for **construction workers**. Construction workers and tradespeople work together to build houses, shops, offices, and roads. Without these workers, people in your community would have no new buildings in which to live and work. Roads would become bumpy and dangerous for drivers.

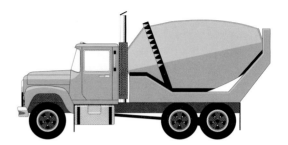

Construction workers do many different jobs, including moving bricks, pouring and spreading concrete, and operating tools and big machines. These workers are making a new driveway.

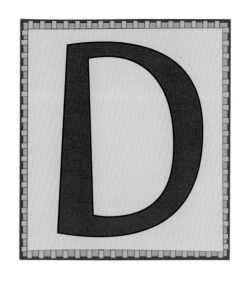

is for **doctors**. Doctors help keep us healthy. They help us get better when we are sick or injured. There are many types of doctors. When people get the flu or need a checkup, they usually visit their **family doctor**. If the family doctor finds a problem that needs special attention, he or she sends the patient to a **specialist**.

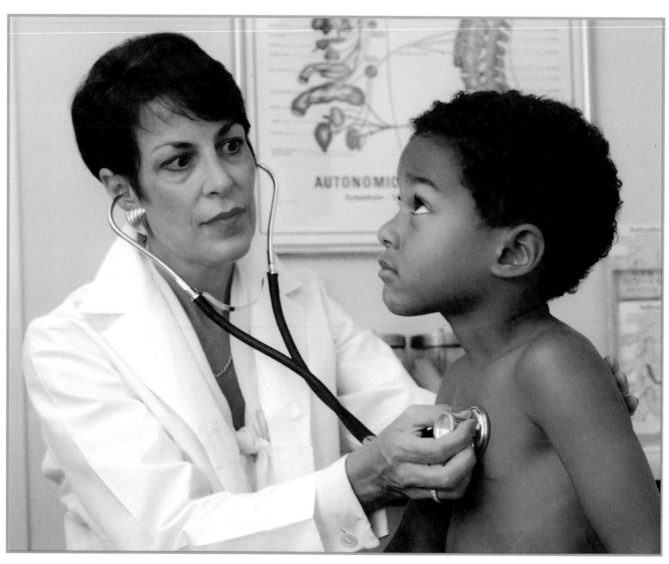

*A **pediatrician** is a specialist who treats children. He or she spends years learning about children's diseases.*

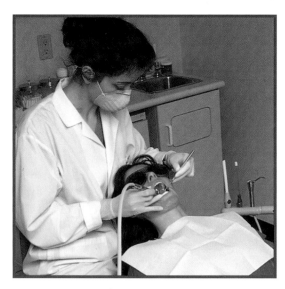

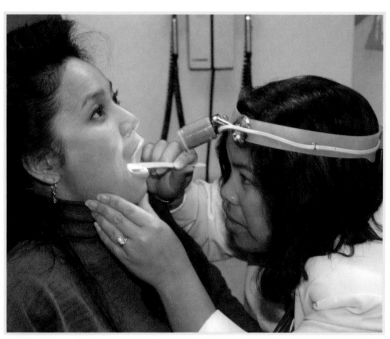

(below) If you have a problem breathing, hearing, or swallowing, you might need to see an **ear**, **nose**, and **throat specialist**.

(above) **Dentists** check teeth, clean them, and put fillings in cavities. They teach patients how to keep their teeth and gums healthy. These twin dentists fix each other's teeth!

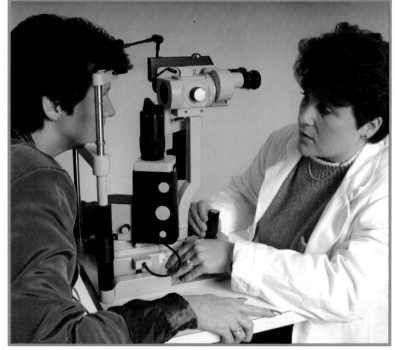

(below) Most doctors put patients' **medical records** on a computer. Medical records help doctors keep track of a patient's illnesses, tests, medications, and treatments.

(above) **Eye specialists** check people's eyes to find out how clearly they can see. When patients do not see well, the eye specialist prescribes glasses or contact lenses to help them see better.

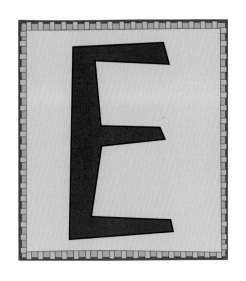

E is for **emergency medical technicians** or EMTs. EMTs drive ambulances or fly helicopters to help people in emergencies. They get people to a hospital quickly. While one EMT treats a patient, the other calls ahead to tell the hospital the patient is on the way. EMTs save many lives every day!

*(right) Many EMTs are **paramedics.** They are not doctors, but they can give patients drugs, put an intravenous in their vein, and use special equipment to treat them for a heart attack. This girl is being taken to a hospital in an ambulance.*

(below) The emergency-room doctors meet the EMT at the helicopter and help him move a patient into the hospital.

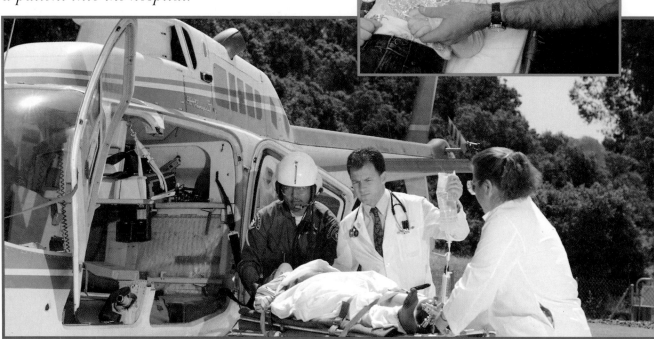

is for **firefighters**. Firefighters put out fires in homes, other buildings, forests, and at car accidents. They rescue people and animals that are trapped by a fire. The smoke and flames from fires are very dangerous. Firefighters risk their lives every time they go to work. Their job takes bravery and special training.

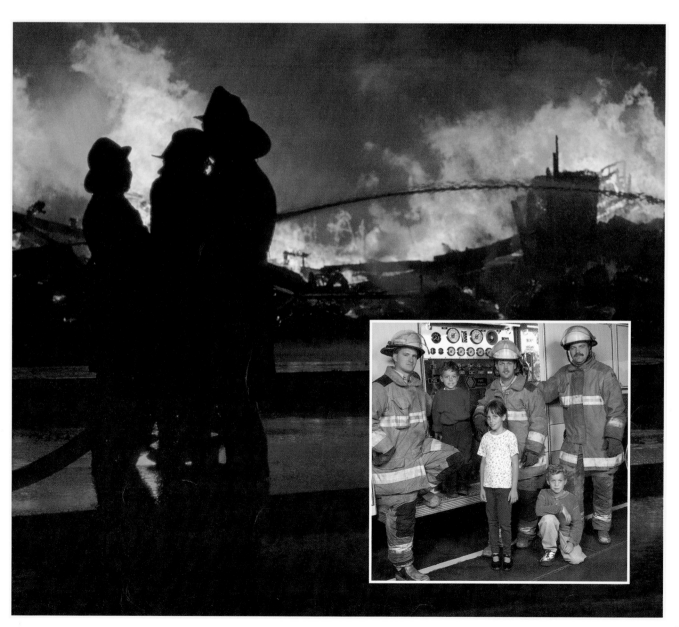

is for **gymnastics coach**. Gymnastics coaches are a type of sports coach. They teach children new gymnastics skills and make sure they do not injure themselves while they are practicing. Sports coaches encourage their athletes to set high goals. They teach children to do their best at everything they try.

*This coach is **spotting**. He stands nearby and makes sure the young gymnast does not hurt himself. He encourages the boy to keep practicing until he knows how to do a move.*

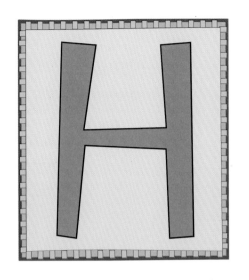

is for **home helpers**. One of the most important parts of any community is the home. A home is where a person lives and feels safe and loved. There are many jobs to do in a home, including laundry, cooking, cleaning, taking out trash, and babysitting. Anyone who does these tasks is a home helper. You can be one, too!

(above) Parents are helpers in and out of the home!
(top left) This boy helps make cookies for the whole family to enjoy.
(left) Many grandparents help raise their grandchildren. People are home helpers when they show their family that they care.

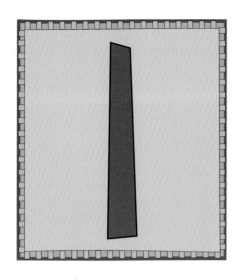

is for **industrial workers**. Industrial workers work in factories where products are made. Many work on an **assembly line**, the part of the factory where things are put together. Assembly-line workers put cars, furniture, and airplanes together a piece at a time. Each worker works on one part or section.

Without industrial workers, we would not have products such as airplanes, refrigerators, and cars. Industrial workers make things that people in many communities use every day.

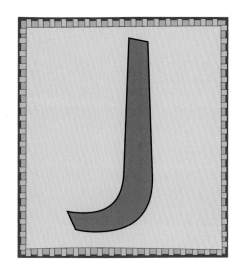

is for **journalist**. People need to know what is happening in their community and around the world. Journalists give them this information. They go to fires, accidents, and special events and **interview** witnesses to get information. They then report about these events in newspapers, magazines, or on television.

Television journalists often take a camera person to an event so they can record it and show other people what happened. The yellow ribbon warns people to "keep out" of the crime area.

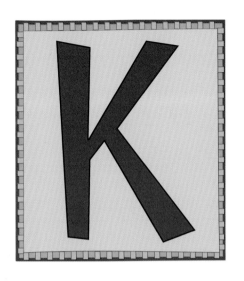

is for **kitchen staff**. A kitchen staff provides meals for people in hospitals, schools, and nursing homes. **Cooks** prepare the meals. In many schools, **servers** in the cafeteria hand students their food. In nursing homes and hospitals, servers put meals on trays and take them to the rooms of patients.

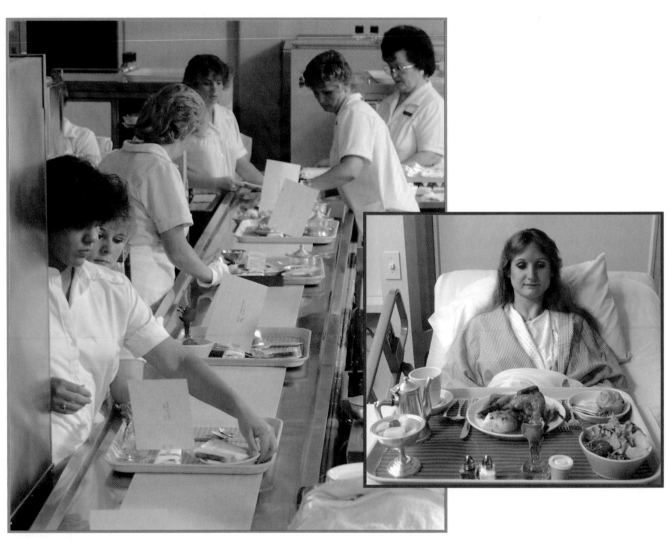

In hospitals and nursing homes, patients cannot cook for themselves. They do not have groceries or a kitchen in their room, and many are too weak or ill to leave their bed. They need the kitchen staff to prepare and serve them nutritious meals.

is for **librarian**. Librarians buy, catalog, and lend out materials to people in a school or public library. You can borrow books, magazines, CDs, and videotapes. If you cannot find a book, a librarian will help you. School librarians also teach you how to use the computer to find information for your projects.

Without libraries and librarians, the people in a community would have to buy more books, magazines, CDs, and videotapes. With a library card, anyone can borrow these things for free. Name all the ways your library and librarian help you and your community.

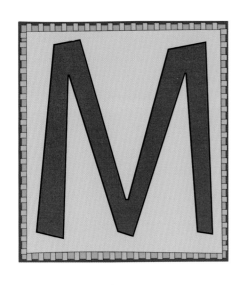

is for **mail carrier**. Mail carriers pick up mail from post offices and deliver it to people's homes and businesses. They must work in all kinds of weather. Mail carriers begin working early in the morning to make sure they reach everyone on their route before the day is done. How often do you receive mail?

Mail carriers help people stay in touch with their friends, family, and customers. They put people's mail in their mailbox. Sometimes they ask people to sign for special letters.

is for **nurse**. Nurses work in nursing homes, clinics, and hospitals. They have many duties. Nurses help make patients comfortable, pass out medicines to them, get equipment ready, and help doctors with operations. Many nurses work in one area of a hospital, such as the emergency or operating room.

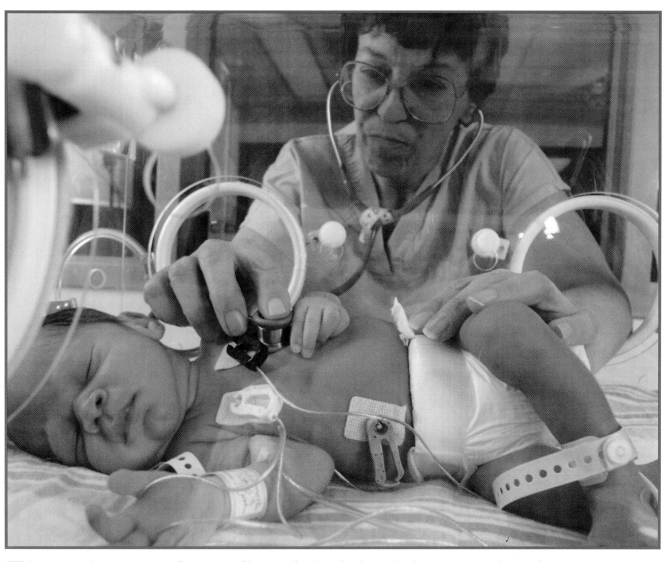

*This nurse is a **neonatal nurse**. She works in the hospital **nursery**, where she cares for newborn babies. She is checking on a **premature** baby. He was born a month early.*

O is for **officers**. Police officers protect and help people in their community. They patrol neighborhoods and watch for people who are breaking the law. They also look out for anyone who needs help, such as a person in an accident or someone who is lost. Some officers patrol highways to catch speeding drivers.

*(inset) Police cars have a radio for calling other police, firefighters, or ambulances. They also receive calls from a **dispatcher** to let them know when they are needed at a crime scene or emergency.*

(above) At an accident, police officers first get medical help for injured people. They then try to figure out how the accident happened by looking at the cars and talking to the drivers and any witnesses who saw the crash.

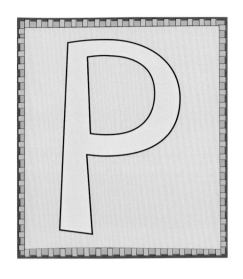

is for **pharmacist**. Pharmacists fill the prescriptions doctors write for us. Pharmacists tell us how to take a drug and what it will do. They must know about thousands of kinds of drugs. They keep track of the medicines we take. Combining some types of drugs can make us sick.

Most pharmacists work in a drug store, hospital, or clinic, where they fill prescriptions. This pharmacist is filling a prescription for a customer with asthma. Other pharmacists work in research laboratories. They do experiments to find new and better drugs.

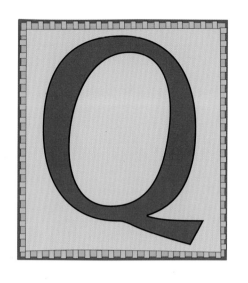

is for **quality-control technician**. Quality-control technicians check products made in factories. Some test new products to make sure they work well and are safe for people to use. Others look for damages to the product before it leaves the factory. Almost everything we buy was checked by a quality-control technician.

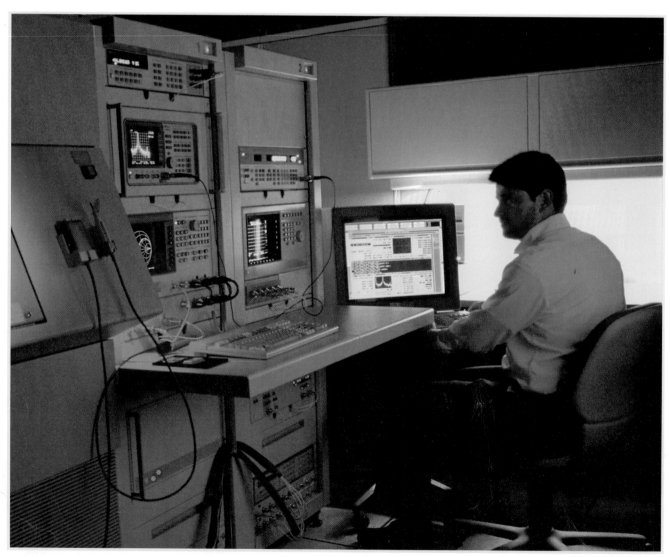

Quality-control technicians often use computers and other scientific equipment to test food, drugs, toys, appliances, and many other products that are for sale in your community.

is for **recycling workers** and **refuse collectors**. Refuse collectors move our trash to landfill sites. Recycling workers pick up paper, glass, and metal items and take them to recycling plants. These workers keep communities clean. Without them, garbage would pile up and attract pests such as rats.

Recycling workers help us help the environment. By recycling metal, glass, and paper, people in a community make less garbage and pollution and save trees.

S is for **service-industry workers**. Service-industry workers make people's lives easier. Customers pay service-industry workers to carry out tasks they do not have time to do themselves or to do jobs that need special skills. These workers include house cleaners, daycare workers, plumbers, mechanics, and taxi drivers.

*This man is a **service advisor** at a garage. He lets a mechanic know what problems a customer has had with a car, and then he advises the customer on what needs to be repaired and how much it will cost. He gets their permission to do the repairs.*

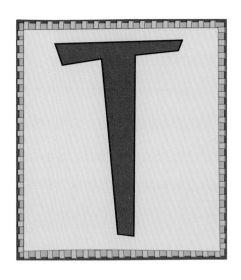

is for **teachers**. Teachers help people learn new facts and skills. Many teachers work in schools. They teach children subjects such as math, history, and science. They also teach students how to read and write. Teachers make learning easier! They explain difficult things in a way that makes them easy to understand.

*This teacher works in an elementary school. There are teachers in high schools, colleges, and universities. There are also teachers who teach people how to use computers or drive. Teachers that teach one skill, such as driving, swimming, or skiing, are called **instructors**.*

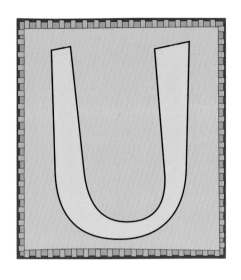

is for **utility workers**. Telephone service, electric power, and running water are called utilities. People need utilities to run their homes and businesses. Some utility workers connect these services to buildings. Others work at the plants that send electricity and water to buildings in the community.

Some utility workers fix problems such as broken phone or power lines that stop services from reaching customers. These workers are repairing power lines high above the ground.

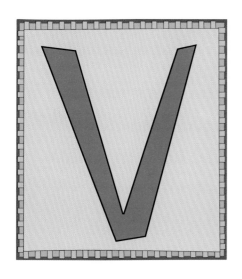

is for **veterinarian**. A veterinarian is a doctor that treats sick or injured animals. People also take their pets to a veterinarian for checkups. Veterinarians give owners advice on how to care for their pets in order to keep them healthy. They also give animals medicine, mend broken bones, and perform operations.

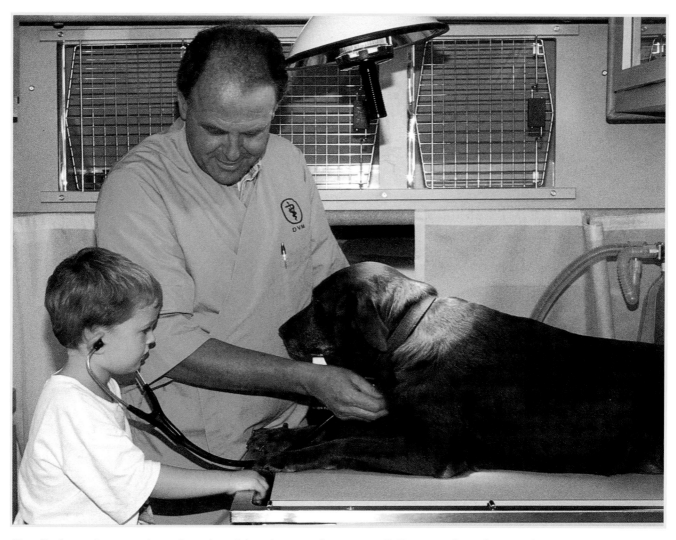

*Dr. Baker, the veterinarian in this picture, has a **mobile veterinarian unit**. It is a big van filled with medical equipment. When someone's animal is ill, Dr. Baker drives his office to where the animal is. He has a very young assistant!*

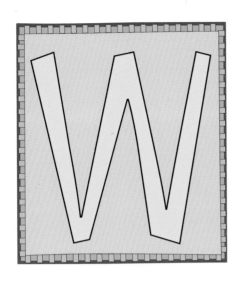

is for **water-treatment workers**. We all need clean water to drink, and water-treatment workers make sure we have it. Used water flows to a treatment plant, where dirt, sewage, and chemicals are taken out of it. Water-treatment workers make sure the water is safe to drink before it goes back to the community.

(above) A water-treatment worker puts a sample in a testing machine. The machine tells him how clean the water is.

(right) The worker looks for dirt in a water sample.

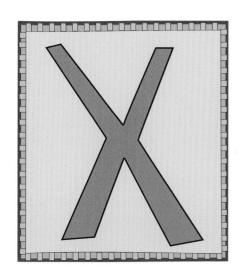

is for **x-ray technologist**. X-ray technologists work in hospitals and clinics. They operate the machines that take x-rays of sick or injured people. X-ray equipment makes images of a person's insides. X-rays can show doctors if their patient has a broken bone, an injured organ, or a cavity in their tooth.

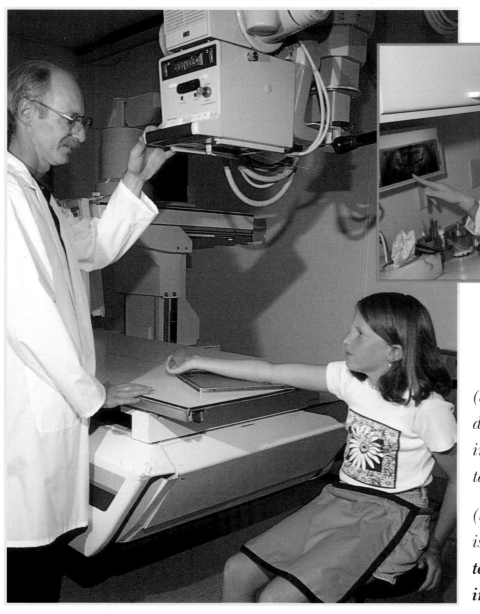

(above) Doctors and dentists examine the images taken by x-ray technologists.

*(left) An x-ray technologist is also called a **radiation technologist** or **diagnostic imaging technologist**.*

29

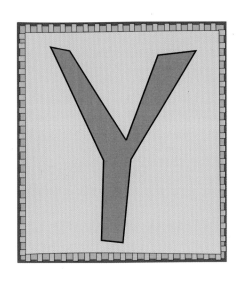

is for **you**. You, too, can be a community helper! There are a lot of jobs you can do to help people in your neighborhood. You could pick up trash from a park or playground. You could go to hospitals or nursing homes to visit people who feel lonely or bored. Remember, anything you do to help is important!

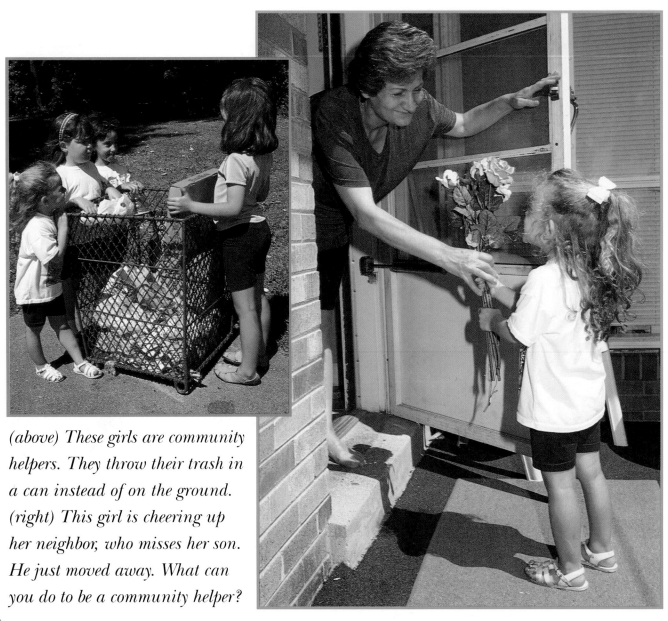

(above) These girls are community helpers. They throw their trash in a can instead of on the ground. (right) This girl is cheering up her neighbor, who misses her son. He just moved away. What can you do to be a community helper?

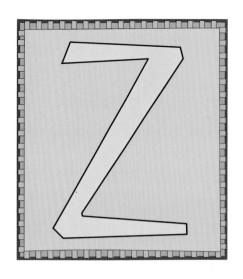

is for **zookeeper**. Zookeepers care for the animals in a zoo. They prepare the animals' food, feed them, and make sure they are healthy. Zookeepers also raise baby animals. Many of the animals in a zoo are endangered in the wild. Zoos and zookeepers help us learn about animals from around the world.

Words to know

asthma A condition that makes a person cough and have difficulty breathing

catalog To record something on a list

community A group of people living in the same area, sharing services and laws

clinic A place, not in a hospital, where people can see a doctor for medical help

dispatcher A person who sends messages quickly to police officers or taxi drivers

endangered In danger of disappearing from the earth

experiment A test done to prove a fact or discover new information

interview To meet with a person in order to ask questions and collect information

intravenous A tube with a needle on the end, which is put into a vein in order to give a patient blood or some other fluid

livestock Animals on a farm

nursery The area of a hospital where babies are cared for

patrol To move around an area in order to guard it and look for problems

prescription A doctor's written order that tells a pharmacist what medicine to sell to a patient

research laboratory A room or building where scientists use special equipment to study a subject or solve a problem

service A business that provides something useful or necessary to a community

sewage Human waste carried by water

tradespeople Workers skilled in a craft or trade such as carpentry

witness A person who has seen or heard an event as it happened

Index

3 4 5 6 7 8 9 0 Printed in the U.S.A. 6 5 4 3 2 1 0 9